BOOKS IN THIS SERIES

BETTER WRESTLING

FOR BOYS

GEORGE SULLIVAN

Illustrated with photographs

G. P. PUTNAM'S SONS • New York

PICTURE CREDITS
Aime LaMontagne, 6, 25, 30; Morgan Sports Products, 20;
New York Public Library, 9. All other photographs are
by George Sullivan.

ACKNOWLEDGMENTS
The author is grateful to the many individuals who
cooperated with him in the preparation of this book.
Special thanks are due Robert Mazzariello, varsity
wrestling coach, East Longmeadow (Massachusetts)
High School, for his help in developing the book's
manuscript and assuring the correctness of the
photographs that appear in it. Special thanks are also
due these high school wrestlers who posed for
photographs: Scott Humphries, Mike Moses, and
Bob Mazzariello of East Longmeadow High School,
and Mark Moynihan of Cathedral High School,
Springfield, Massachusetts. The author is also grateful
to Doug Parker, wrestling coach of Springfield
College, for granting permission to use the wrestling
facility there for photographs; to Francesca Kurti,
T.L.C. Custom Labs; Herb Field, Herb Field Art
Studio; Aime LaMontagne; and Bill Sullivan.

Published in 1989 by G. P. Putnam's Sons, a Division of The
Putnam & Grosset Group, 200 Madison Avenue, New York, N.Y.,
10016. Originally published in 1986 by Dodd, Mead & Co., Inc.
Published simultaneously in Canada.
Printed in the United States of America.

Library of Congress Cataloging-in-Publication Data
Sullivan, George, 1927–   Better wrestling for boys.
SUMMARY: Discusses the history, weight classes, equipment,
moves, and holds of boys' wrestling, and explains how team
competition works. 1. Wrestling—Juvenile literature.
[1. Wrestling]   I. Title GV1195.S825 1989 796.8'12
88-32392   ISBN 0-399-61237-8

4   5   6   7   8   9   10

CONTENTS

Both strength and mobility are necessary for wrestling success.

A CLASSIC SPORT

Wrestling is one of the most popular of all school sports, and it's becoming more popular every season.

It's not hard to understand why. Struggling hand-to-hand while attempting to pin an opponent's shoulders to the mat is an activity in which just about any boy can excel.

You don't have to be particularly big, as in football. You don't have to be taller than average, as in basketball. Thanks to wrestling's system of weight classification, you always compete against someone who is your size, or very close to it. Indeed, in wrestling, a small kid can be a big star.

Today, wrestling ranks as the fifth largest school sport—behind football, basketball, track and field, and baseball.

Most boys first become interested in competitive wrestling in junior high or high school. Coaches agree that the best time to be introduced to the sport is between the ages of twelve and fifteen.

Some beginners start wrestling earlier, in elementary school. The United States Wrestling Foundation offers competition for 9- and 10-year-olds in the organization's Kids Division.

The USWF also has programs for youngsters ages 11-12 and 13-14. These programs are active in 35 states. They include the U.S. Kids' Championship and the National Junior Championship.

The style you develop as a wrestler may depend to some extent on your build. If, for example, you're tall and lanky and have good flexibility, your coach may want you to become a leg wrestler. In leg wrestling, the objective is to overcome the opposition by using a variety of scissors moves in which you lock your legs around your opponent's body.

If, on the other hand, your upper body is powerfully built, you will probably want to put an emphasis on learning holds and throws that demand strong arms and shoulders.

No matter the type of build you have, strength is essential. You can become stronger through weight training, following a program that stresses repetitions (rather than one that concentrates on the amount of weight lifted). Calisthenics and running can also help you to improve your general physical condition.

Another requirement is mobility. You have to be capable of deft movement anytime you step onto the mat to face a competitor.

Many of the other skills that wrestling demands are described and pictured in this book. They are skills that can be learned through practice and good coaching.

There are many variations of these skills, however, as well as an enormous number of moves and maneuvers. It would take a book the size of the Manhattan telephone directory to explain them all.

Why wrestle? Why not concentrate on some simpler, less-demanding sport?

There are several reasons. When you wrestle in competition, you must be in topflight physical condition. As you may have already discovered, when you're at a physical peak, you look better and feel better.

Wrestling is also valuable because it teaches self-discipline and self-reliance. Self-discipline is a "must" in conditioning yourself and learning wrestling's basic moves.

As for self-reliance, that's an essential ingredient anytime you face an opponent. During a match, when you begin to tire, your coach is not going to send in a substitute for you. Substituting is not allowed. In wrestling, you're always on your own.

Yet wrestling also offers all the benefits of a team sport. Any wrestler will tell you that having your teammates clap you on the back after a winning match is one of the joys that makes the training grind worthwhile. Yelling for your teammates from matside during competition and traveling with them to distant cities for meets or tournaments are some of team wrestling's other pleasures.

Most important, wrestling can't help but build your confidence and increase the respect you have for yourself. "It's a sport in which any boy, no matter his size, can be a varsity competitor, win a letter, and even become a state champion," says Bob Mazzariello, varsity wrestling coach at East Longmeadow High School in East Longmeadow, Massachusetts. "A boy can win great respect from his peers through wrestling—and this has got to help him throughout his life."

AN ANCIENT SPORT

Like running, throwing, or jumping, wrestling is one of the most natural of all sports. And like the others, it dates to the earliest of times.

Wrestling is known to have existed some 5,000 years ago. On the walls of temple tombs in Egypt's Nile Valley, archaeologists have found simple drawings that depict more than 200 wrestling holds, all of which are known to wrestlers today.

Wrestling was introduced into the Olympic Games in 704 B.C. The sport is mentioned in the Bible several times.

After the Romans conquered Greece, they blended their own style of wrestling with the earlier form the Greeks used. The result was Greco-Roman, which has lasted to this day. In Greco-Roman, wrestlers are not permitted to use their legs to hold or trip an opponent, nor are they permitted to use any holds that involve the opponent's legs or hips.

In European countries at the beginning of the Christian era, wrestlers had a lofty status. Many monarchs of the time took their greatest pride in having a powerful army. But their next greatest possession was a champion wrestler.

Even before that period, wrestling was well known in many Asian countries. Japanese sumo wrestling, in which bouts are usually decided in a few seconds, is still practiced today.

German wrestlers of the sixteenth century

The American Indians wrestled well before the arrival of Columbus. The early Spanish settlers had their wrestlers, as did the Dutch and English colonists and the French in Canada.

According to the U.S. Wrestling Foundation, seven American presidents were wrestlers—George Washington, Zachary Taylor, Andrew Jackson, Abraham Lincoln, Ulysses S. Grant, William Howard Taft, and Theodore Roosevelt.

At the time Lincoln wrestled, the American "catch-as-catch-can" style was in favor. Catch-as-catch-can, in contrast to the traditional Greco-Roman style, permitted a wrestler to grab any part of an opponent's body. Only the stranglehold, a hold across the throat which choked off an opponent's breath, was barred. Real rough-and-tumble matches were often the result.

When the Amateur Athletic Union (AAU) was formed in 1888, wrestling was divided into professional and amateur competition. Weight classes (see Chapter 3) were established.

In its early years, professional wrestling was almost as honorable and upright as the Boy Scouts. But in the years following World War I, the sport began a downhill slide. Today, professional matches are no more than exhibitions, with performers displaying as much acting skill as wrestling ability.

The participants wear outrageous costumes. Usually a "good guy" is pitted against a "bad guy." Every pro match follows a script that is carefully worked out in advance. Holds and punches are faked. Even the length of bouts is predetermined. Wrestling is an honest sport only on an amateur level.

Today, there are two principal forms of wrestling —freestyle, which developed from catch-as-catch-can, and Greco-Roman. In freestyle, opposing wrestlers attempt to throw each other to the mat and secure holds that score points or which enable them to pin their opponent's back to the mat. A wrestler is permitted to apply holds on his opponent's legs and use his legs to trip or throw an opponent. He can also use his legs to apply holds.

Freestyle is the type of wrestling featured in junior high and high school competition. It is also used in college competition, although college and high school freestyle rules are not exactly alike.

Some college wrestlers also compete in Greco-Roman. The Amateur Athletic Union (AAU) conducted the first national Greco-Roman championships in 1953.

In the Olympic Games, competition is held under international rules in both freestyle and Greco-Roman. These rules are somewhat different than those that govern American collegiate wrestlers. Despite this, American wrestlers made a splendid showing in the 1984 Olympic Games. In twenty wrestling classes, Americans won thirteen wrestling medals, including nine golds. These included two gold in Greco-Roman, a stunning development, since the U.S. had never won a Greco-Roman medal in Olympic competition before.

It must be said that the Americans' medal total might not have been so great had teams from such wrestling powers as the Soviet Union and Bulgaria been present. Both countries boycotted the 1984 Olympics. Nevertheless, no one disputes the fact that the United States is now an important force in international wrestling competition.

WEIGHT CLASSES

To eliminate the unfairness of a big man wrestling against an opponent who is not so big, wrestlers are divided into weight classes. In high school and junior high school competition, there are twelve weight classes. They are:

98 pounds
105 pounds
112 pounds
119 pounds
126 pounds
132 pounds
138 pounds
145 pounds
155 pounds
167 pounds
185 pounds
Heavyweight

The minimum weight for a wrestler in the 98-pound class is 83 pounds. The maximum weight for a heavyweight contestant is 275 pounds.

The rules also provide growth allowances. In other words, it is expected that you will grow and add poundage during the season (roughly from December through March), and you are legally permitted to do so. This applies, no matter what your weight class happens to be.

You're allowed a growth allowance of two pounds between December 25 and February 1, an additional pound between February 1 and March 1, and another pound after March 1—a total of four pounds for the season.

In which weight class should you compete? There is no easy answer to that question.

Let's say you weigh 114 pounds. It would seem appropriate for you to compete in the 119-pound weight class (which includes wrestlers from 113 to 119 pounds). But most wrestlers prefer to wrestle "down," that is, to wrestle in the lowest possible weight class. For example, a boy who weighs 114 pounds might seek to reduce his weight to 109 or 108 pounds so that he would be eligible to compete in the 112-pound class. The theory is that he will be able to make a stronger showing in the lower weight class.

Some coaches, however, advise their wrestlers to wrestle "up," that is, compete in the next *higher* weight class. When you do this, it's not likely that you'll have to worry about "making" weight. Of course, your matches will be tougher because you'll be competing against bigger boys. But tough competition won't hurt you. It will help to make you a better wrestler.

Let your coach advise you as far as your weight class is concerned. Perhaps your school has a trainer you can also consult. He might be able to perform certain tests that can establish how much body fat you have. You can then determine the amount of weight you can safely lose.

If you are carrying around some extra pounds, you might want to shed them. Cutting back on the number of calories you're taking in while increasing your physical activity is the safe way to lose excess poundage.

Whether or not you're attempting to lose weight, your diet should focus on those foods that are high in nutritional value. The foods you eat should include:

• Eggs, meat, poultry, and fish for protein and minerals.

• Leafy green vegetables (spinach, lettuce, cabbage), yellow vegetables, and peas for vitamins and minerals.

• Citrus fruits, apples, cherries, grapes, plums for vitamin C and roughage.

• Potatoes and similar root foods for starch, vitamins, and minerals.

• Cereals and cereal grain breads for energy vitamins and minerals.

• Butter or margarine (in moderate amounts) for vitamin A and oil.

• Water, tea, sugarless lemonade, buttermilk, clear soups, or bouillon to replace body fluids.

Your state wrestling association will require that you and other members of your team be certified at a specific weight by a specific date. You cannot be recertified at a lower weight during the season.

All wrestlers must weigh in before competing. The referee or other authorized person conducts the weigh-in. If your weight is not within the limits of your class, you will not be permitted to compete in that class.

Some wrestlers have to resort to frantic weight reduction methods to make weight for a match. Abstaining from all food and drink is one such method. Running in a rubber or vinyl suit or using a sweatbox are others. Such activities can seriously endanger your health. The rulesmakers have taken note of this and have put a ban on such activities as running in a rubber or vinyl suit, using a sweatbox, hot shower or whirlpool for weight reduction. Nor are wrestlers permitted to use drugs in an effort to lose weight.

You shouldn't have to starve yourself, indulge in very strenuous workouts, or rely on some bizarre form of activity to make weight. The better choice is to move up to the next higher weight class.

HOW A MATCH IS SCORED

In high school competition, a wrestling match consists of three periods, each two minutes in length, making the entire bout six minutes. (In college competition, matches are eight minutes long, consisting of a two-minute opening period followed by two three-minute periods.) There is no rest time between periods.

A referee is on the mat with the wrestlers. He is in charge of the match. He judges whether holds are legal, awards points that are earned by the wrestlers, signals when one wrestler has scored a fall, and halts the match should one or both wrestlers go out-of-bounds.

In tournament competition, the referee may be helped by an assistant referee or mat judge. Other officials include a timekeeper and a scorekeeper.

Before the match, you will be designated as either the "red" or "green" wrestler, and given a red or green elasticized band to wear on your ankle. Red designates members of the visiting team; green, the home team.

The referee and the scorekeeper are not likely to know your name or recognize your school colors as represented by your uniform. The distinctively colored anklet band helps them in identifying you during the match. For example, if you're a member of the visiting team, and have just earned a takedown, the referee will award you your (two) points by shouting out, "Two, takedown, red!"

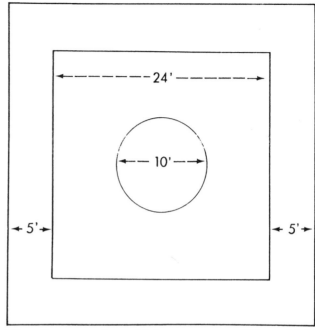

Wrestling area is a 24-foot square within which there is a 10-foot circle. Area is surrounded by a safety mat that is 5 feet wide on each side.

All action takes place on a mat usually made of plastic cellular material. The mat's wrestling area must measure at least 24 feet on each side. When the wrestling area is circular in shape, the circle must be at least 28 feet in diameter.

At the center of the mat is a circle that is 10 feet in diameter. Within the circle are the starting lines. These are parallel lines that are 3 feet in length

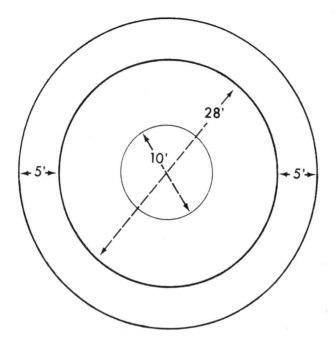

Wrestling area can also be circular in shape, with a 28-foot circle enclosing one that is 10 feet in diameter. A safety mat, 5 feet wide, surrounds the outer circle.

and 12 inches apart. They are connected by a red line at one end (to be used by the "red" wrestler) and by a green line at the other end (for the "green" wrestler).

In the first period of a match, you and your opponent meet in the center of the mat, shake hands and then assume an upright stance as you await the referee's whistle that starts the action. (You also shake hands after the match.)

Suppose you've been designated the "red" wrestler. One foot must be on the red starting line. The other foot must be on the line, too, or behind it. (Most wrestlers position one foot behind the other.) You are not permitted to place either foot in front of or outside the starting line.

The second and third periods begin with your opponent taking what is called the referee's position. In this, one man assumes the defensive starting position, or bottom position. He is on his hands and knees, with the knees behind the rear starting line. His palms are flat to the mat and forward of the front starting line.

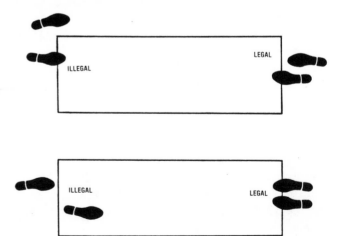

In the second and third periods, action begins from the referee's position.

The other man takes the offensive starting position, or top position. He sets himself to the right or left of the bottom man, one knee to the mat. One arm encircles him. (Chapter 11 describes these positions in detail.)

A coin toss determines which wrestler has the choice of position. If you win the toss and take the top position at the beginning of the second period, your opponent will automatically be awarded the top position at the start of the third period, and you'll have the defensive position. Again, action begins with the referee's whistle.

15

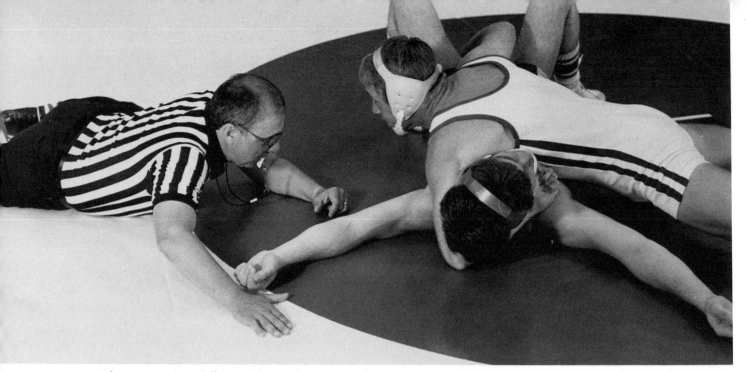

Referee signals a fall, or pin, has been scored.

When you're the wrestler on top, your goals should be to register a takedown (see below), to ride your opponent, that is, to maintain control of him and, thus, to tire him out and pin him.

When you're the bottom wrestler, your objective should be to achieve an escape, then ride your opponent, tire him, and go for a pin.

The rules also provide for optional starts. For instance, the offensive wrestler can, if he chooses, merely place his hands on the defensive wrestler's back.

The offensive wrestler does not even have to kneel. He has the option of being able to stand behind the defensive man and place his hands on the man's lower back.

The No. 1 objective in any match is to defeat your opponent either by a pin (also called a fall). A pin immediately ends the match. You can also win by outscoring your opponent under a point system.

A pin occurs when you're successful in holding your opponent to the mat on his back with his shoulders or scapulas in contact with the mat for two seconds. ("Scapula" is a word you'll hear often in wrestling. It refers to the back part of the shoulder, the shoulder blade. The plural is sometimes spelled "scapulae.") Anytime you score a fall, you win the match, no matter what the point score happens to be at the time.

As this suggests, a fall is something like landing a knockout punch in boxing. And, like the knockout punch, a fall can occur at any time.

The winner in most matches is decided on the basis of points. Wrestling's point system is as follows:

TAKEDOWN—2 points

You register a takedown when, from a neutral position, you "take" your opponent to the mat, then keep him on the mat until the referee determines you have control over him.

REVERSAL—2 points

This is a move in which you go from a defensive position to one in which you control your opponent. In other words, you "reverse" roles with him.

ESCAPE—1 point

A maneuver in which you go from a defensive position to a neutral position.

NEAR FALL—2 points

A near fall occurs when you place your opponent in a pinning situation, momentarily holding both of his shoulders or scapulas within approximately four inches of the mat. A near fall also occurs when you press one of your opponent's shoulders or scapulas

to the mat while the other shoulder or scapula is held at an angle of 45 degrees or less with the mat.

NEAR FALL—3 points

If you can hold either of the near-fall positions described above for five or more consecutive seconds, you earn 3 points.

To earn a pin, you must hold your opponent's shoulders or scapulas—shaded areas—to the mat for at least two seconds.

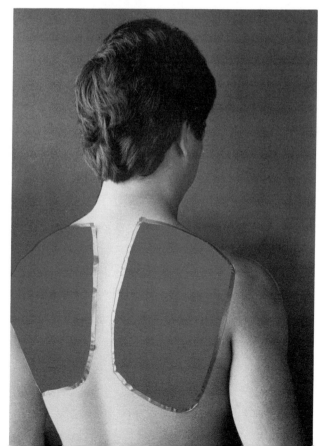

There is also a system of penalty points. For breaking a rule, you, the offender, are penalized 1 or 2 match points. These points are added to the score of your opponent.

You can be penalized for such technical violations as assuming an incorrect starting position, going off the wrestling area, grasping your opponent's clothing, or leaving the mat without permission.

Unnecessary roughness or stalling can also cause you to be penalized. Stalling is called when the referee judges a wrestler is not wrestling offensively and avoiding contact with his opponent.

Certain holds are illegal. These include any stranglehold, the twisting hammerlock, neck wrench, full nelson, and several others.

You cannot twist or force an opponent's head or any limb beyond its normal limit of movement. You cannot twist fingers, toes, or ears—any flesh. Striking blows of any kind is also forbidden.

Naturally, all action must take place within the boundary lines marked on the mat. But sometimes the wrestlers spill over the line. If you and your opponent go beyond the line with neither of you holding an advantage, the match will be restarted in a neutral position.

Suppose one man has the advantage when the wrestlers go off the mat. The referee stops the action, the wrestlers return to the center of the mat and take the referee's position. The wrestler that held the position of advantage at the time the two men went out-of-bounds assumes the top position.

Merely having a part of your body outside of the boundary line does not necessarily mean that you are legally out-of-bounds. The rules state that a wrestler is still considered to be in bounds if his supporting points remain within the boundary line. A wrestler's supporting points are those that bear his weight. For example, when a wrestler is down on the mat, his usual supporting points are his hands, knees, buttocks, and the side of his thigh.

Let's say that as you are attempting to pin an opponent, he manages to get his head and shoulders out-of-bounds. You can still pin the man, since his supporting points remain inbounds.

For a complete rundown on the rules, obtain a copy of the "Official High School Wrestling Rules." The rulebook is available from the National Federation of State High School Associations (11724 Plaza Circle, Box 20626, Kansas City, Missouri 64195). It costs $4.50 ($2.50 plus $2.00 for shipping and handling.)

EQUIPMENT

Wrestlers sometimes wear tight-fitting sleeveless shorts and shirts or full-length jersey tights. A one-piece, jersey-style uniform, known as the singlet, is now very popular. The singlet is cooler; it gives greater freedom of movement.

Shoes for wrestling are heel-less, light in weight, and reach above the ankle. They're usually made of nylon.

Pick shoes that have padding at the ankle and are

High-top wrestling shoes should give you traction on the mat when you need it.

Singlet is preferred over other types of wrestling uniforms.

durable. The outsoles should give you traction when you need it but should not hinder your movement on the mat in any way.

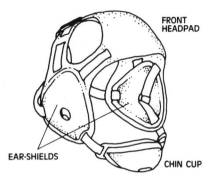

FRONT HEADPAD

EAR-SHIELDS

CHIN CUP

Headgear protects the ears, offers padding at the chin, and often the forehead.

Don't wear basketball shoes for wrestling. The outsoles are not designed for use on the mat and could lead to injury.

You must also wear protective headgear that covers the ears. An adjustable, buckle-free strap holds the headgear in place during a match. Before such protection was required, wrestlers often suffered from "cauliflower ear." This is a condition in which the ear becomes reddened and misshapen by repeated injury. Headgear also protects against rupture of the eardrum.

Lightweight kneepads are optional. They've become quite popular in recent years. Kneepads, like headgear, must fit snugly and stay in place during a match.

In staggered stance, one foot is slightly ahead of the other.

TAKING YOUR STANCE

At the beginning of a match, you and your opponent will be on your feet and facing one another in what is called a neutral position. You're each trying to score a takedown.

Your body position should provide you with the greatest possible power and mobility. Keep your chin up, your back straight. Bend slightly at the knees and waist.

Get your hands out in front of your body, ready to grasp your opponent. Bend your arms slightly.

21

Keep your elbows close to your hips.

Your feet should be spread about shoulder-width apart. Carry your weight on the balls of your feet; don't be flat-footed.

In your starting position, you can use either a square stance or a staggered stance. Choose the one that gives you the greatest freedom of movement, both for launching an attack or defending yourself.

Most wrestlers use a staggered stance. In this, the feet are spread so as to provide solid balance, with one foot slightly ahead of the other. In the square stance, the feet are spread, again providing good balance, but neither foot is forward; the toes are even.

The advantage of the staggered stance is that it makes it easier to defend yourself. Since one leg is in front of the other, you know which leg your opponent is going to shoot for. And you virtually eliminate the double-leg takedown (see Chapter 10) as one of your opponent's weapons.

The advantage of the square stance is that it enables you to move from one side to the other with greater ease.

In square stance, neither foot is forward.

22

HOW TO MOVE

You must learn to move quickly and smoothly on the mat, whether you are circling your opponent or moving into or away from him.

When you're moving to your right, step first with your right foot. When you are moving backward, step first with the back foot. Use short, quick steps.

If you follow this advice, one foot will never cross in front of the other. You'll be off-balance and vulnerable to attack anytime your feet cross.

When you want to turn fast, use a pivot step. Suppose you want to turn to the right. Concentrate your weight on your right foot, lift your left foot, then pivot on the right. You should be able to pivot as much as 180 degrees, turning your body from front to back.

When you're moving about, be sure to maintain the proper body position. Keep your chin up. Bend slightly at the knees and waist.

Don't extend your arms or lean forward from the waist. Don't do anything that gives your opponent the opportunity to grasp you in a hold.

Your movements must be quick and deft. Keep your chin up; bend at the knees slightly.

23

HOW TO LIFT

Lifting is a vital skill. You must be able to lift quickly and decisively in taking down an opponent or when applying a pinning move. Lifting is also crucial in countering a takedown or when seeking to escape.

Anytime you lift an opponent, you take away his supporting base. Without that base, he can't muster any power; it's not easy for him to counterattack.

Your strongest muscles are in your legs and thighs. These are the muscles you must use to lift effectively.

Anytime you plan a lifting move, first bend at your knees; lower your hips.

As you drive toward your opponent, be sure to keep your hips low. Get your hips under him as you grasp him with your arms. Then straighten up, hoisting the man into the air. Don't lift with your arms. Don't lift with your back. Get under your opponent and let your hips and thighs do the work.

Left: Keep low as you drive toward your opponent; get under him.

Right: Then straighten up, hoisting him into the air.

This basic tie-up involves getting one hand behind your opponent's neck and, with the other hand, maintaining inside arm control.

TIE-UPS

A tie-up is a preliminary move that leads to a takedown. Several tie-ups are described and pictured in this section. No matter which tie-up you're attempting, you must move quickly and decisively. That's the key to success.

It's not necessary to use a tie-up to score a takedown. You can "shoot your move" directly from your stance. Wrestlers in the heavier weight classes, where strength is a more important factor than quickness, are more likely to rely on a tie-up to set up a takedown attempt.

As you and your opponent confront one another, keep your chin up and back straight. Your chest should be positioned over your knees.

What you don't want to do is lead with your head and upper body as you move in. Do so and you can be quickly subdued with a side headlock or other hold.

And don't reach with your hands. You then become an easy target for an arm drag, with your

With one hand behind your opponent's neck and the other gripping his wrist, you establish a collar-wrist tie-up.

Here's how to achieve wrist control of your opponent.

opponent grabbing one of your wrists, sliding his other hand under your armpit to grasp your upper arm, then yanking you to the mat.

Three of the most frequently used tie-ups are as follows:

COLLAR TIE-UP WITH INSIDE ARM CONTROL—Clamp one hand behind your opponent's neck. With the other hand, grasp the inside of his arm just

above the elbow.

COLLAR-WRIST TIE-UP—Again, place one hand behind your opponent's neck. Use the other hand to grasp his wrist.

DOUBLE-WRIST TIE-UP—This is exactly what the name suggests. Gain control of your opponent by getting a firm hold on both of his wrists.

TAKEDOWNS

When the referee's whistle blasts to begin the match, your strategy should be to grapple for position and go for a takedown. "Set 'em up and take 'em down" is the way you hear this expressed.

You register a takedown when you "take" your opponent to the mat and get him under control. A takedown is worth 2 points.

The wrestler who achieves the first takedown of a match, and thus wrestles with a 2-point edge, holds a big psychological advantage. And it looms bigger and bigger as the seconds slip away.

Your coach may teach you as many as 10 or 15 different takedown moves. You'll probably be expected to become skilled in the use of only three or four of these moves, or variations of them.

Keep in mind that the best wrestlers are sometimes known for favoring only one or two moves. What makes them the best is that no one can stop them from using the moves successfully.

SINGLE-LEG TAKEDOWN—On a high-school level, 90 percent of all takedowns are achieved by either the single-leg or double-leg takedown. The single-leg takedown is the most common of the two. Because it is used so frequently, many wrestlers are adept at defending against it. You have to move quickly and aggressively in order to be successful with the maneuver.

In this and most other takedown attempts, you

To achieve a single-leg takedown, get down low as you drive in.

29

Moving in a circular direction, lift, then drive your opponent to the mat.

launch your attack with a penetration step. This gets you inside your opponent's defenses and close enough to make a decisive move.

When attempting a single-leg takedown, take the penetration step toward the side you're attacking. For example, if you're attacking your opponent's left leg, step to the outside of his left leg with your right foot.

Keep your chin up as you step. Keep your back straight. Keep your arms close to your hips until you're in position to grasp the opponent's leg.

Don't make the mistake of lowering your chin and bending at the waist as you move in. Remember, the proper way to get down low is to bend at the knees so as to lower your hips. As before, keep your chin up, your back straight.

And don't make the mistake of reaching for your opponent while you're still a good distance

away. This could enable him to grab your hands or arms and smother your attack.

As soon as you've clamped onto the other man's leg, lift the leg into the air to get him off-balance or use the leg to drive him to the mat. You'll be moving in a circular direction. As you lift and drive, be sure you're using the big muscles of your hips and thighs.

DOUBLE-LEG TAKEDOWN—The double-leg takedown, when executed aggressively and with precision, can send your opponent to the mat in a hurry. However, the double-leg takedown can be a

The double-leg takedown begins with an aggressive penetration step. Grasp your opponent tightly, lift, then topple him backwards onto the mat.

In executing the high-crotch single-leg takedown, first clear your opponent's arm out of the way. Go in low, grasp tightly, lift.

difficult move to execute because your opponent is likely to be looking for it and alert to defend against it.

Again, trigger your attack with a decisive penetration step. This time thrust your lead foot between your opponent's feet.

Drop to one knee and encircle your arms across the back of your opponent's thighs. Lock your hands together, if you can.

Drive your shoulder into your opponent's body. Lift him into the air and spill him backwards onto the mat.

HIGH-CROTCH SINGLE-LEG TAKEDOWN—With the high-crotch single-leg takedown, you attack your opponent's hips rather than his legs. It's a maneuver that requires plenty of speed as you penetrate, and a quick finish.

To set up the high-crotch takedown, it's likely you'll have to clear one of your opponent's arms from the area of attack. Push the arm inward and upward so that you can get in close.

Penetrate by means of a lead step with your outside foot. If you're attacking his right hip, step with your left foot. Keep your chin up as you go in; lower your hips. You must, in fact, get your hips lower than your opponent's.

A lift is used to finish the high-crotch takedown. If your opponent gives ground, get your arms around his hips. From that hold, you can finish the move as you would the double-leg takedown.

In attempting the head-and-heel takedown, first get control of your opponent's head. (See opposite page.) Then get down low and reach with the other hand to grasp his heel. Last, spill him backwards.

HEAD-AND-HEEL TAKEDOWN—This move is usually attempted off of a tie-up, the collar-inside arm tie-up (Chapter 9).

While keeping control of your opponent's head, drop to your knees. At the same time, reach to grasp your opponent's near heel. Then pull hard,

toppling him to the mat.

It's important to grasp behind the *heel*, not behind the calf or thigh. By grasping the heel and pulling, you eliminate your opponent's power base. Grab higher on the leg and he'll be able to resist your move.

CROSS-ANKLE PICK—This is a simple but effective maneuver, especially if your opponent makes the mistake of letting his weight rock him back on his heels.

As in the case of the head-and-heel takedown, you must get control of your opponent's head before you attempt to grab his ankle.

While keeping control of his head, wheel him around, forcing him to take a step with his outside foot. As he does so, drop to one knee and grab the outside ankle. Pull up on his heel and down on his head and spill him to the mat.

This move, like many in wrestling, is circular in the direction it takes. By moving your opponent in a circle, you bring his foot (or arm or shoulder) into your grasping range.

While a takedown is very important, it shouldn't be your ultimate goal. Once you've gained control of your opponent, attempt to apply a pinning combination that enables you to score more points. Pinning combinations are explained in Chapter 12.

In executing the cross-ankle pick, again you must first establish head control. Then grab your opponent's outside ankle, pull up on the heel, and tumble him to the mat.

Wrestlers in referee's position

BREAKDOWNS

The second and third periods of every match begin with both wrestlers in the referee's position. This is also the position used to restart a match after the wrestlers have gone out-of-bounds.

In the referee's position, one man is designated the defensive wrestler. He is the bottom man. He is down on his hands and knees, with his knees behind the rear starting line. The heels of his palms are flat to the mat and forward of the front starting line.

The offensive wrestler takes his starting position to the right or left of the defensive man. One arm goes around the defensive wrestler's body, and the hand is placed loosely over the defensive wrestler's naval. The top man places the palm of his other hand—his near hand—over his opponent's elbow.

The top man must have at least one knee to the mat on the near side of his opponent. His head must be above the midline of his opponent's body.

When the whistle sounds, the man on top strives to break down his opponent. The bottom man goes for an escape on reversal (Chapter 13). Most wrestlers, incidentally, are more successful at escaping and reversing than they are at riding or breaking down their opponents.

When the referee flips the coin to decide who will be the top man and who will be on the bottom, which should you choose? To a great extent, it depends on the strategy your coach is using. Coaches often prefer that their wrestlers choose the top position in the second period, hoping the wrestler will at least be able to ride out his opponent, if not break him down. Then, in the third period, when he's assigned the defensive position, he can go for an escape.

The theory here is that you'll be less tired in the second period than in the third; you'll be stronger. So the second period is the best time to take on the more difficult task of riding and breaking down.

Riding doesn't mean simply hanging on until the clock runs out. The best way to ride is by constantly applying pressure with breakdown moves and pinning combinations. If you keep the bottom man busy defending, he won't have time to attempt an escape or reversal.

The score of the match also must be considered when choosing the up or down position. Is your team ahead or behind? If your team is trailing, how many points are needed to take over the lead?

The best advice is to consult with your coach. Discuss what strategy he plans.

As mentioned earlier, when you're on top, your goal is to break your opponent down—to flatten him to the mat—before he can escape or reverse you.

Edward Clarke Gallagher, an outstanding coach at Oklahoma A&M University (now Oklahoma State), and sometimes called the "father" of American wrestling, often noted that being successful in

the top position was based on a simple principle. He compared the bottom wrestler to a table with four legs. If you take away one of the four legs and apply force, the table falls. If you remove two or more legs and apply force, it falls more easily.

This principle underlies all breakdowns. Remove a point of support—a hand, foot, or knee—and apply pressure, and you'll break your opponent down.

When the whistle sounds, you, the top man, should get your hips as close to the bottom man's hips as possible. This helps to prevent him from using his hips in executing an escape move.

When you lean into the bottom man, you force him to use his hands for support. This makes it difficult for him to gain hand control. Breakdowns develop from this position.

Here are three simple breakdowns.

FAR-ANKLE, FAR-KNEE BREAKDOWN—From the offensive starting position, the top position, reach with your right hand to grasp your opponent's far ankle. At the same time, reach under your opponent's midsection with your left hand, gripping his far knee.

As you drive your shoulder into his ribs, pull him

To execute far-ankle, far-knee breakdown, reach to grasp your opponent's ankle with one hand. Attack the base of his knee with your other hand. Pull him toward you, spilling him to the mat.

toward you—"suck him in"—and break him down.

Once you've achieved this breakdown—or any breakdown—you must control your opponent until you apply a pinning combination, forcing his shoulders to or near to the mat.

FAR-ANKLE, CROSS-FACE BREAKDOWN—This is similar to the far-ankle, far-knee breakdown described above. But this time, as you grasp your opponent's far ankle, you also reach across his face to take hold of his far elbow. Keep him controlled with your chin and upper body.

Last, pull him toward you, toppling him onto his back.

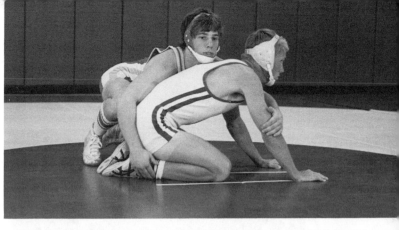

This is the far-ankle, cross-face breakdown. Grasp your opponent's far ankle with one hand and reach across his face to take hold of his far elbow with your other hand. Pull him over onto his shoulders.

HEAD-IN-ARM BREAKDOWN—Drive the top of your head into your opponent's near shoulder. At the same time, take hold of his near wrist with your left hand. Then drive him forward, breaking him down.

Once you have your opponent's shoulder pinned to the mat (with your head), any one of several other moves are possible. You can, for example, lift his arm and place it behind your head. Pushing backwards, you spin him over onto his shoulders. Then quickly move in for the pin.

The head-in-arm breakdown can also lead to a bar arm (in which you use your arm as a lever, or "bar," to turn the man over), then a half nelson and a pin. These pinning combinations are described in the next chapter.

In executing the head-in-arm breakdown, drive your head into your opponent's near shoulder. At the same time, get control of his near arm. Then drive forward, crunching him to the mat.

In executing the half nelson, get your left hand under your opponent's left arm and across the back of his neck. Also keep control of his right hand.

To get him on his back, swing your body around until it is perpendicular to his. Tighten the hold. Get up on your toes and force him over.

PINNING COMBINATIONS

Merely breaking down your opponent doesn't win you any points. You have to get him under control, and seek to press his shoulders or scapulas to the mat.

The pinning combinations described in this section are meant to give you the leverage you need to do this. Your objective, of course, should be to try to register a fall or score near-fall points, or "back points," as some wrestlers call them.

Several pins belong to the nelson family. The term "nelson" refers to any hold in which pressure is placed on the back of an opponent's head by reaching under one of his arms with one of your arms, or under both of his arms with both of your arms. (When you do use both hands and arms, you're executing a full nelson, which is an illegal hold in amateur wrestling.) Nelsons are extremely effective in achieving pins.

HALF NELSON—The half nelson is often used following a breakdown. As the bottom wrestler at-

In executing the three-quarter nelson, you lock your hands. Your right arm goes under your opponent's body; the left hand comes from the other direction. Then pull down on the man's head, forcing him onto his back.

tempts to raise himself, get control of his right arm with your right hand and thrust your left hand under his armpit and across the back of his neck. The higher up on his neck that you place your hand, the more leverage you'll get.

Once the half nelson has been applied, swing your body in a clockwise direction until it is perpendicular to his, then drive forward. As the bottom man starts going over onto his back, tighten the hold. Get yourself chest to chest with him. Spread your feet to distribute your weight over a bigger area and dig in with your toes to increase your leverage.

THREE-QUARTER NELSON—The three-quarter nelson is a hold in which you put pressure against the back of your opponent's head with both of your hands and arms, one from below, the other from above.

The hold can be used almost anytime during a match. It's often applied from the referee's position. Let's say you're the wrestler on top; you're positioned on the left side of your opponent. His head is down; his weight is forward.

Place your left forearm across the back of his neck. Thrust your right arm around his body and then under it. Lock your hands.

Pull down on the man's head. At the same time, encircle his near ankle with your outside foot. Then walk the leg around, putting him on his back.

NEAR-SIDE CRADLE—Cradles are popular pinning maneuvers in which you, the top wrestler, wrap your arms around one of your opponent's legs and his head, and then turn him over onto his back.

Let's say that you're in the referee's position and

Begin the near-side cradle by reaching with your left hand past your opponent's head. Thrust your right hand behind his near knee. Lock your hands. Then drive your head into the man's rib cage and lift the knee, driving him onto his back.

In executing the cross-face cradle, reach with your left hand beneath your opponent's chin to grasp his triceps. Thrust the other hand behind his right knee. Grasp your left wrist with your right hand, and roll him over.

set up on the left side of your opponent. Shoot your right hand behind his left knee. At the same time, reach in the other direction with your left hand. Lock your hands across the back of his neck.

To finish the move, drive your head into your opponent's rib cage and lift his left knee into the air, forcing him over onto his back.

CROSS-FACE CRADLE—Again, let's assume you are set to your opponent's left in the referee's position. Reach with your left arm across his face, and grasp his right triceps (the muscle at the back of the upper arm). With your other hand, reach behind his right knee. Start rolling him over.

Next, grasp your left wrist with your right hand. Keep rolling the man over until you've got him on his back.

DOUBLE-TROUBLE PIN—This hold is sometimes called the double overhook. It begins from a position in which your opponent is flat to the mat, stomach down.

Thrust your left hand beneath his left arm. Your right hand goes beneath his right arm. Lock your hands.

Lift the man's near arm and shoulder, turning the man onto his back into a pinning situation. The chances are very slim that he'll be able to escape.

To get your opponent in a double overhook, get your left hand beneath his left arm, and your right hand beneath his right arm. Lock your hands. Then, driving from your toes, force him over.

49

ESCAPES AND REVERSALS

Takedowns, breakdowns, and pins represent only one side of the coin. You also have to be skilled in escapes and reversals.

You seek to escape or score a reversal anytime you and your opponent are in the referee's position and you're the bottom wrestler.

An escape occurs when you are able to free yourself from the top man's control and achieve a neutral position. An escape is worth 1 point.

A reversal is better. When you are able to register a reversal, you go from a position of disadvantage to one of advantage, from a bottom position to a top position. In other words, you take control. A reversal earns 2 points.

Becoming highly skilled in escapes and reversals can win you a big tactical advantage. For example, you may have seen matches in which one of the wrestlers deliberately chooses the bottom position. He knows that he's going to be able to escape and score a takedown, thus adding 3 points to his match score. (Scoring a takedown from the top position is worth only 2 points.) "Let him up and take him down" is how this strategy is described.

Several escapes and reversals are described in this section. All begin from a solid base. Spread your knees apart. Keep your chin up, your buttocks down.

Your weight should be evenly distributed on your hands and knees. If you lean in one direction or another in anticipation of a move, you're tipping off what you plan to do, and thus handing your opponent the advantage.

It's also important to control your opponent's hands. If you don't do this, he can apply any one of a variety of holds and keep you tied up. Some coaches say that no principle is more important than hands control in becoming a successful bottom wrestler.

Speed and explosive power are vital. For example, a well-known escape move is the Oklahoma stand-up. At the sound of the whistle, the bottom wrestler explodes into action. His head and hands go up; his back arches. With a sudden wrench of his torso, he pops to his feet, throwing off the top man as if he were a bath towel. You may not have the strength or experience to attempt the Oklahoma stand-up, but it typifies the type of movement that is required when you're the bottom man.

STAND-UP—The stand-up is used to escape more frequently than any other move. If it doesn't accomplish an escape, it can trigger other moves that lead to escapes or reversals.

Let's say that your opponent is positioned to your left side. Grab your opponent's right hand to control it. Shove your weight back into his body.

Get your left foot on the mat and explode your body upward.

As you get to both feet, pull your opponent's right hand off your waist. Use both hands. Then turn toward him. You're now in a neutral position.

In executing the stand-up, get your left foot to the mat, then explode upward. At the same time, you must control your opponent's hands; otherwise, you won't be successful.

In achieving a sit-out escape, get your right foot to the mat, then your left, so you're in a sitting position.

SIT-OUT—This move, like the stand-up, must be executed quickly and decisively.

Let's say that your opponent is again positioned to your left. After gaining control of his right hand, thrust your weight back into his body.

Get your right foot to the mat and raise yourself upward. Slide your left foot out, so that you come to a sitting position. Be sure to keep your elbows

Flip over onto your knees, then launch your attack.

tight to your body so your opponent can't slip his hands under your arms and pull your shoulders toward the mat.

You can't stay in a sitting position for more than a split second. Quickly execute a tight shoulder roll, turning onto your knees and coming head to head with your opponent. Then reach to grasp him about the waist.

53

HOOK AND ROLL—A roll is a good way to trigger a reversal. This one begins when you, the bottom man, reach back with your right arm to hook your opponent's right arm. Pull the arm down and turn in toward him, bringing his chest tight to your back. Then start rolling to the right, hauling your opponent with you.

Once you've completed the roll, look for an opening that permits you to apply a pin.

A variation of this maneuver is to grip and control your opponent by his wrist, and then roll.

To score a reversal by means of a hook and roll, first get control of your opponent's right arm, then roll onto your right shoulder, flipping him over as you go.

In achieving a switch, twist your body to the right, getting into a sitting position against your opponent.

Then reach around to grasp his far side . . .

. . . pulling yourself to the top position.

SWITCH—The switch is another move that can be used to produce a reversal. There are several different types. This one begins when you abruptly twist your body to the right, moving your left hand far to the right as you do so. (This gets the hand beyond the top man's reach.) Now you're up against your opponent in a sitting position.

Reach over his body and grasp the top of his thigh with your left hand. Flatten him out. This is achieved by the leverage you exert on your opponent's shoulder. Get on top of the man. You end up with your chest against his back, pressing him to the mat. This is a difficult maneuver but it can produce devastating results.

TEAM COMPETITION

In most parts of the country, the wrestling season extends from November or December to March or April. During the season, you and your teammates are likely to compete anywhere from 20 to 30 different times.

Your team will be made up of one wrestler from each of the twelve weight classifications that are listed in Chapter 3.

Competition is of two types—dual meets and tournaments. Most of your competition will be in the form of dual meets, whereas championships will be decided in tournaments.

A dual meet is competition between two teams. Each team's score is the sum of the scores of the individual members. Competition begins with the lightest weight wrestlers and works up to the heaviest.

Team points in a dual meet are awarded as follows:

Fall	6 points
Forfeit	6 points
Default (because of injury)	6 points
Disqualification	6 points
Decision (see below)	
• by 12 or more points	5 points
• by 8 through 11 points	4 points
• by less than 8 points	3 points
Draw	2 points

One wrestler registers a decision over another by outscoring him in bout points (as explained in Chapter 4). A decision by 12 or more points over one's opponent is called a superior decision and earns the winning wrestler's team 5 team points. A decision of 8 to 11 points is called a major decision and earns 4 team points. Decisions of less than 8 points are worth 3 points to the team. As all of this implies, your margin of victory over your opponent can be as important to your team as the victory itself.

For you, as a competitor, tournaments are much different than dual meets. In a dual meet, you participate in only one match. But in a tournament, you are likely to be matched against several competitors in one day. The maximum number of matches in one day for one competitor is five. There must be at least 45 minutes of rest between matches. Endurance is thus as important as skill in tournament competition.

Another distinctive feature of tournaments is that there are no draws. All ties are settled by overtime periods. In high school tournaments, the overtime consists of three one-minute periods. Competition begins from the referee's position. There's a one-minute rest period between the end of regulation time and the beginning of the overtime.

Two judges and the referee watch the overtime. If there is still a tie after the overtime, these three officials vote for a winner on the basis of aggressiveness and overall offensive prowess.

Referee signals match winner.

Tournaments are usually single-elimination or double-elimination. In the single-elimination tournament, competing teams are paired in individual rounds. The winners advance to the next round and losers are eliminated until there is a single champion.

In a double-elimination tournament, a team must lose twice before being eliminated.

Most tournaments involve a number of teams that is divisible by 4—4, 8, or 16 teams. This enables the competing wrestlers in each weight division to move from the first round to the final matches in an uninterrupted sequence.

If there are too few competitors in any one weight class to compete in a grouping of 4, 8 or 16, some wrestlers receive a bye. Should you be awarded a bye, you automatically advance to the next round without competing.

Your ambition doesn't have to be to win every match in which you're entered. You don't have to become the state champion. Your goals can be quite modest.

Perhaps you've lost a match to a highly skilled and experienced wrestler. He pinned you. If beating the man the next time you face him seems impossible, your goal can be not to let yourself get pinned. Or if the wrestler defeated you by a 10-0 score, say, when you meet him again, simply try to score points.

Do your best; try to learn from your mistakes. What's important is to participate, sharing in the fun and excitement of competition. Winning is something extra.

GLOSSARY

ARM DRAG—A move in which one wrestler grasps the wrist and upper arm of his opponent and pulls the arm across his body, yanking him to the mat.

BOTTOM POSITION—*See* Defensive starting position

BREAKDOWN—A move by which a wrestler in the offensive position flattens his opponent by knocking a hand or knee out from under him.

BYE—The position of a competitor in an elimination tournament who has no opponent after the participants have been paired, and who is advanced to the next round without having to compete.

CATCH-AS-CATCH-CAN—An early type of freestyle wrestling in which competitors were permitted to use any type of hold except the stranglehold.

COUNTER—A wrestler's move to thwart an opponent's move and turn it to his advantage.

CRADLE—A maneuver in which the top wrestler wraps his arms around his opponent's neck and leg, then locks his hands, to achieve a pin.

DECISION—The awarding of a match to the wrestler with the most points when there is no fall.

DEFAULT—The failure of an individual to continue wrestling for any reason, resulting in a win being credited to his opponent.

DEFENSIVE STARTING POSITION—The position of the wrestler who is on his hands and knees at the beginning of the second or third period, or whenever the referee calls for a restart of the match. The heels of his palms are flat to the mat and forward of the front starting line. Knees must be behind the rear starting line.

DISQUALIFICATION—To bar a contestant from competition for infractions of the rules.

DOUBLE-ELIMINATION TOURNAMENT—A wrestling tournament in which a team must lose twice before being eliminated.

DUAL MEET—Competition between two teams in a series of matches, one in each of a series of weight classes. Each team's score is the sum of the scores of individual members.

ESCAPE—To gain a neutral position after having been controlled by one's opponent. In a match, an escape is worth 1 point.

FALL—*See* Pin

FREESTYLE—A style of wrestling in which opposing wrestlers attempt to throw one another to the mat and to secure holds which score points or which enable them to pin an opponent's back to the mat.

FULL NELSON—An illegal hold in which one wrestler reaches with both hands under his opponent's arms from behind to put pressure on the back of his head.

GRECO-ROMAN—A style of wrestling in which competitors are not permitted to use their legs in any active manner (as in tripping an opponent or applying a scissors), nor are they permitted to use any holds that involve the opponent's legs or hips.

HALF NELSON—A hold in which one wrestler reaches under his opponent's arm from behind, pressing his hand against the back of the man's head.

MAJOR DECISION—In a dual meet, a decision by 8 to 11 bout points over an opponent. A major decision is worth 4 team points.

MATCH—Competition between two wrestlers.

NEAR FALL—A situation in which one wrestler momentarily holds both of his opponent's shoulders or scapulas within four inches of the mat. A near fall also occurs when one wrestler presses one of his opponent's shoulders or scapulas to the mat while the other shoulder or scapula is held at an angle of 45 degrees or less with the mat.

NELSON—A hold in which leverage is placed against the back of an opponent's

neck or head by reaching under one or both his arms.

NEUTRAL POSITION—The position from which the match begins, with neither wrestler in control. Both wrestlers are at the center of the mat, in a slight crouch and facing one another. Their hands are in front of their bodies at or just above waist level.

OFFENSIVE STARTING POSITION—The position of the wrestler who is at the right or left side of his kneeling opponent at the beginning of the second or third period or whenever the referee calls for a restart of the match. One knee is on the mat and his head is above the midline of the opponent's body. One arm goes around the bottom man's body and the hand is placed loosely over his navel. The palm of the other hand goes over the defensive man's elbow. Also called the top position or position of advantage.

OPTIONAL START—When wrestlers are in the referee's position, the decision by the man in the offensive starting position merely to place his hands on the defensive wrestler's back.

OUT-OF-BOUNDS—In a match, when the supporting points of both wrestlers are outside of the mat boundary lines.

OVERTIME—In tournament wrestling, the three one-minute periods after the end of a match that has ended in a tie.

PENALTY POINT—The point awarded to one wrestler when his opponent is judged to have broken a rule.

PIN—To hold an opponent to the mat on his back with his shoulders or scapulas in contact with the mat for two seconds. A pin, officially called a fall, wins the match in dual competition.

POSITION OF ADVANTAGE—See Offensive starting position

POSITION OF DISADVANTAGE—See Defensive starting position

REFEREE'S POSITION—A kneeling position taken by both wrestlers to start the second or third periods of a match or to resume action after it has been halted by the referee. See Defensive starting position, Offensive starting position.

REVERSAL—A maneuver in which a wrestler goes from a defensive position to one of control.

RIDING—When wrestlers are in the referee's position, maneuvering by the top wrestler in an effort to maintain control of the bottom wrestler.

SCAPULA—Either of the two large, flat, triangular bones forming the back part of the shoulders; the shoulder blade.

SCISSORS—Any one of a number of holds in which a wrestler locks his legs around his opponent's head or body.

SIDE ROLL—A reversal maneuver in which the bottom wrestler rolls to his right or left, carrying the top wrestler with him, and gaining opportunity for a pin.

SINGLE-ELIMINATION TOURNAMENT—A wrestling tournament in which opposing teams compete in individual rounds. Winning teams advance to the next round and the losers are eliminated until there is a single champion.

SINGLET—The one-piece jersey-type uniform worn by wrestlers.

SIT-OUT—An escape move from the referee's position in which the bottom wrestler gets one foot to the mat, then the other, pushes himself into a sitting position, and then rolls over to grasp his opponent about the waist.

STALLING—The failure to wrestle aggressively, avoiding action.

STAND-UP—An escape move from the referee's position in which the bottom wrestler gets one foot to the mat, then thrusts his body to a standing position.

STARTING LINES—The pair of parallel lines at the center of the mat used by wrestlers in taking their starting positions. The starting lines are 3 feet long, 12 inches apart, and connected at the ends.

SUMO—Traditional Japanese form of wrestling.

SUPERIOR DECISION—In a dual meet, a decision by 12 or more bout points over an opponent. A superior decision is worth 5 team points.

SUPPORTING POINTS—The parts of the wrestler's body that bear his weight and are in contact with the mat, including

his hands, feet, knees, sides of the thighs, and buttocks.

SWITCH—A reversal move from the referee's position in which the bottom wrestler turns and reaches back to secure a hold on his opponent, gets on top of him, and presses him to the mat.

TAKEDOWN—Taking an opponent to the mat and gaining control over him.

TECHNICAL FALL—A fall that is awarded when one wrestler has earned a 15-point advantage over his opponent.

THREE-QUARTER NELSON—A hold in which one wrestler puts pressure on the back of his opponent's head with both hands, one from below, the other from above.

TIE-UP—When wrestlers are in a neutral position, a preliminary hold that leads to a takedown.

TOP POSITION—*See* Offensive starting position

U.S. WRESTLING FEDERATION—The national governing body of amateur wrestling.